Dream Walls

Dream
Walls

An Inspirational Guide
to Wall Coverings

CHARLES T. RANDALL
MELANIE BYSOUTH

RANDALL INTERNATIONAL

Published in the United States by:

Randall International

Orange, California

Distributed in Great Britain by:

Antique Collectors Club Ltd

Woodbridge, Suffolk

First Edition

ISBN 1-890379-07-7

How to reach us:

Phone: (714) 771-8488

Toll Free: (800) 882-8907

Internet: http://www.randallonline.com

Editor-in-Chief: Melanie Bysouth

Illustrated by: Burgandy Beam and Bradley Clark

Photo Editor: Melanie Bysouth

Text and Layout: Melanie Bysouth

Cover Design by: Diego Linares

Library of Congress Cataloging-in-Publication Data

Randall, Charles T.
    Dream walls : an inspirational guide to wall coverings / Charles T. Randall, Melanie Bysouth.
        p. cm.
    Includes bibliographical references and index.
    ISBN 1-890379-07-7 (hardcover)
    1. Wall coverings. I. Bysouth, Melanie Irene, 1973- II. Title.
    NK2115.5W3 R36 2004
    747'.3—dc22

                                                                                                2004007605

10 9 8 7 6 5 4 3 2 1

CONTENTS

Historical Wall Coverings   8-31

Renaissance, Baroque, Early Georgian and Rococo, Neoclassic and Late Georgian, Federal, Empire and Regency and Victorian

Wallpaper   32-75

Country Inspired, Floral, Tropical, Vintage, Illusional, Ornamental, Understated, Opulent, Striking, Expressive, Youthful, Animated, Refined, Extravagant, Gothic, Fanciful, Striped, Checkered, Dynamic, Elegant, Simple, Exotic, Geometric, Abstract, Romantic and Modest

Paint   76-109

Pink Odyssey, Hushed Rose, Purple Royalty, Granite Sea Agate, Lemon Zest, Splish Splash Cyan, Arcadian Blue, Lavender Twilight, Carnation Pink, Forest Floor, Prelude Blue, European White, Blush Champagne, Aquatic Mist, Orchid, Scarlet's Velvet, Coral Sunset and Fresh Mango

Stone and Tile   110-141

Bluffstone, Cliffstone, Country Rubble, Fieldledge, Hillstone, Limestone, Mountain Ledge, River Rock, Rustic Ledge, Shadow Rock, Stacked Stone, Top Rock; Ceramic Tile, Porcelian Tile, Faux Stone, Textured Surfaces, Chiseled Finishes, Metallic Highlights, Listellos and Chair Rails

Wood Paneling   142-175

Raised Panels, Beadboard Panels, Recessed Flat Panels, Modern Flat Panels, Wainscoting, Natural, Medium, Dark, Paintable, Maple, Cherry, Oak, Mahogany, Walnut and Anigre

Alternative Wall Coverings   176-213

Unique Shelving, Built-In Aquariums, Sculpture, Creative Architecture, Wall Flowering, Rustic Log Walls, Fabric, Creative Furnishing, Murals, Brick, Faux Finishes, Artistic Partitions and Accents, Hi-Tech Diversions, Eclectic Fusion, Quadrilateral Design and Creative Room Division

Designer's Portfolio   214-263

Wallpaper Catalog   264-269

Paint Catalog   270-275

Source Guide   276-279

Glossary of Terms   280-283

Index and Bibliography   284

INTRODUCTION

One could suppose that wall decor began in the Old Stone Age, when prehistoric man used charcoal and manganese to create images of mammoths, horses and bison on cave walls.

Or perhaps it was during the New Stone Age when Egyptian artists painted images on the walls of tombs.

For the origins of faux finishing, one could look to the Romans who, around 90 B.C., used paint to replicate costly marble and stone and, from 80 to 15 B.C., offered the illusion of columns or works of art.

One may return to prehistoric times to find the first use of tapestries as wall coverings or leap ahead to the 1500s to discover the first wallpaper. Yet no matter when and where wall coverings began, it is impressive to see what they have become.

Contemporary wall design allows wallpaper to tantalize the imagination and paint to bring a room to life. It reveals brilliant opportunities for stone and divulges innovative concepts for tile. It gives wood paneling a subtle elegance that awakens the simplest of rooms and it permits one's creativity to explore endless possibilities.

As you turn the pages of Dream Walls you will quickly see why it is the only wall book you will ever need. It begins with a beautifully illustrated look at historical wall coverings and proceeds to consider wall design from the most simple to the most dramatic. Tradition is both accepted and questioned while obtuse design is all but forgotten.

And it cannot be denied that the detail of modern wall design is a representation of its rich and vibrant history.

NOTES ON THE WALLPAPER AND PAINT
CATALOGS AND THE SOURCE GUIDE

Once the pursuit for the perfect wall covering is complete, countless hours are often consumed with the search for the colors and patterns found in the photograph that inspired you. Along with stimulating your creativity for design, Dream Walls also gives you the information you need to make your new room concept a reality.

Throughout the Wallpaper chapter you will find small squares that highlight the detail in the various photographs. These squares can also be found in the Wallpaper Catalog, in the back of the book. Each square in the Catalog is accompanied by the manufacturers name and the name of the wallpaper. Contact information can be found on the first page of the Source Guide.

For each of the images in the Paint chapter, corresponding squares of paint can be found in the Paint Catalog, in the back of the book. Each paint color that is featured in a photograph will be represented in the Paint Catalog, along with the manufacturers name and the name of the paint. Contact information can be found on the first page of the Source Guide.

Lastly, for images found in the Stone and Tile, Wood Paneling and Alternative Wall Coverings chapters, as well as the Designer's Portfolio, simply turn to the Source Guide, find the page number of the photograph you have selected, and you will see the complete contact information for the creator of the design.

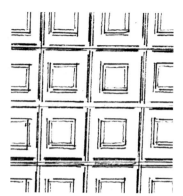

Renaissance 1400-1649

Beginning in Italy in the 1300s, the Renaissance period signaled a rebirth of the spirit and culture of ancient Rome and Greece. In the 1420s, there was a resurgence of Roman architecture and with it, a desire to create structures that built upon the ideas of classical antiquity.

In private homes, the most important rooms were those that could be seen by passersby and more often than not, ornately decorated with simple colors. It was quite popular for walls to be adorned with the illusion of stone or marble as the beginnings of modern day faux finish came to life. Wood paneling was also a wall covering of choice and could be either

unfinished or painted, yet plaster walls would rarely be seen without a coat of paint.

Textile wall hangings were also popular in rooms striving to make a statement. Yet it was only in the homes of the very rich that tapestries would be found. The 16th century saw the domination of gilded leather hangings along with what was perhaps the father of wallpaper as small panels of printed paper were adhered to the wall. Expressive wall decoration, such as mirrors and paintings, became common in the late 1500s, along with maps that often hung in halls and reception rooms. The Spanish Renaissance also allowed for grand embellishment of simple, plaster walls. Brightly colored tiles could be found on the walls and stairways. Upper class homes would often display elaborate hangings made of silk, velvet and damask. Known for its leatherwork, Spain demonstrated its talent on walls of gilded leather. In the kitchen, a fresquera, a decorative food cabinet, would often be seen hanging from the wall.

Gothic detail is perhaps the greatest distinction of the French Renaissance. This was most prominently seen in the tall wood paneling that featured Gothic-inspired carvings or paintings. Much like the Italians, the French embraced the illusion of stone during the Renaissance period. Yet French homes included textiles in their elegant faux finish. Embellished fabric was often seen, as were tapestries. It was around this time that wallpaper made its first appearance though it only did so in the homes of the merchant classes. For those who could not afford expensive tapestries and textiles, wallpaper proved a perfect substitute.

The English Renaissance also experienced the birth of wallpaper and much like in

France, the aristocrats were not yet ready to embrace it. For the upper classes, oak wood paneling, sometimes carved to resemble hanging linen, was quite popular. As the period progressed, so did the opulence of the panels.

Color was the rage and was often eccentric though simple colors were used when hoping to give the suggestion of wood paneling or marble. Yet white was not out of the question and was frequently the choice when a wall was to be covered with a great tapestry. Along with paint, plaster walls were also adorned with quadrilateral designs or images depicting mythological or biblical tales. Wallpaper did begin to gain in popularity toward the end of the period yet not until it became more lavish, and therefore, more expensive.

Baroque 1643-1730

In the 17th century, Europe was consumed with the styles and concepts of the Baroque period. It was an era during which design attempted to blend architecture, furniture and design in a single theme. It was known as a movement that stepped away from the classicism of the Renaissance as it stepped toward the reflection of the religious and political ideals of the time. Baroque made its start in Rome and quickly spread throughout Europe yet it was not as popular in Protestant nations such as Holland and England who held tight to the ideals of the Renaissance. Possibilities were limitless as nothing was too much in the Baroque Era. Inspired by Catholicism and the Monarchy, churches, homes and buildings became larger than life with the architecture and design to match. Overwhelming arches and ornate wall carvings could often be seen. Bright, vibrant colors including red, blue, green and purple were prominent as were gilded finishes. Myriad textures of the period included both real and faux finish marble and stone, stuccowork

and wood paneling. In many homes, dadoes were painted in rich colors or adorned with paneling. The remaining two thirds of the wall was often an extension of the dado yet for the wealthy, the wall could be covered with expensive tapestries, fabric or leather. Ornately framed mirrors also came into great popularity as did elaborate oil paintings yet these too were mostly reserved for the upper classes.

Incorporating the trompe l'oeil techniques of the Renaissance, the Baroque period saw royal palaces as a dramatic canvas. Frescoes, paintings created on damp plaster, quite literally embedded the walls with the artist's masterpiece. As the plaster set, it permanently bound the colors to the wall allowing for a work of art to become virtually eternal. Images depicted in the artwork included both biblical and mythological ideals.

Chinese wallpaper entered Europe courtesy of the Baroque period as the hand-painted detail perfectly represented the affluence of the era.

Known more commonly as Louis XIV, the Baroque period enveloped France as an homage to its leader. With a strict focus on the King, the ideals of the Louis XIV period evoked the wealth and power of France and were thereby limited to the aristocracy.

Luxury and color were prominent in the era as was dramatic grandeur and a sense of awe. Adding to the blues, reds, greens and purples of Italian Baroque, the French included white and gold in their elaborate decor. Walls often centered around intricate fireplaces that were commonly adorned with marble. Mirrors and paintings, often sitting in gilded frames, were also common and could sit atop a mantel or hang across from a window. Wood paneling followed strict quadrilateral (four-sided) design and was sometimes accompanied by a mural. Textiles came into play as wall hangings and included expensive silks and velvets. Remaining one of the more costly decorating choices, tapestries, which often depicted the life of the King, remained limited in their appearance.

As the 18th century began in France, so did the Rococo period. Breaking away from the formality of the Baroque era, design became light, whimsical and asymmetrical. Catholicism and the Monarchy were replaced with an exploration of romantic and pastoral life. Though, much like the Baroque period, Rococo maintained a blending between decoration and furniture, it did so with simplicity virtually nonexistent in the years before.

Just over a decade later, as England was being introduced to its new king, George I, Britain was undergoing remarkable changes in both architecture and design. With the revival of Palladian architecture, a style created by Italian architect Andrea Palladio, came a strange blending of French Baroque, Franco-Dutch Baroque and Neo-Palladian. The result, Palladian, was a style far more classical than the new Rococo that had developed in France. Combine that with the simplicity of the Anglo-Dutch-influenced Queen Anne style, the Rococo, Chinese and Gothic-inspired Thomas Chippendale and the eventual arrival of French Rococo and the

Early Georgian period can perhaps best be described as all encompassing.

It was during the period known as French Regency that the ideals of Rococo began to soften the opulence and grandeur of Baroque. Rooms became smaller, as did decoration, and asymmetry replaced strict, rigid lines. Wood paneling began to take the place of marble and columns were no longer the fashion. Though Rococo was fast becoming the style of the era, its simplicity remained unwanted in the most important of rooms where luxury was still the order.

Colors also made the transition from French Regency to Rococo as gilded white was replaced with pastel yellows, blues and greens.

Not following all the ideas of Rococo, wood paneling remained symmetrical though it was traditionally softened with rounded edges and arched corners. Ornamentation and carving had been given new freedom and was no longer limited by molding and borders. Paneling was often covered with fabric or painted with an embellishment of flowers, foliage and fruits. Tapestries, still limited in their appearance, displayed Rococo themes in brilliant color. Wallpaper, both hand-painted Chinese and flocked English, was popular and was often used to give the illusion of textiles. Mirrors became prominent and could be found in great number throughout a home. No longer restricted to the walls, mirrors could be encountered on window shutters, above and inside of fireplaces and on ceilings. As an eclectic blending of styles, the Georgian period commenced with the return to classical and Baroque ideals. Rooms could not be too big, furniture could not be too extravagant, colors could not be too bold and fabrics could not be too expensive. For smaller

DREAM WALLS

homes, the Palladian style was scaled down yet it still retained the hints of the Renaissance seen in the grandest of homes.

By the 1750s, wallpaper, textiles, fireplaces and furniture began to seek influence from French Rococo, Chinese and Gothic styles. Soon after, English Rococo was developed as a much more conservative alternative to its predecessor.

The Georgian period, much like French Rococo, began with an embracing of wood paneling, traditionally recessed but often raised in the homes of the wealthy. Rooms intended for the most important of guests could feature gilded paneling or detailed cornices. Sometimes, paneling would include shelving whose shape reflected antique collectables of the era.

By the middle of the 18th century, wood paneling had been replaced with ideas thought more stylish. Fabric and plaster-work became a common sight in homes. Damask, silk, velvet and tapestry each had their place in the Early Georgian period. Hand color-washed and blocked wallpapers allowed for yet another design option.

Wallpaper could imitate fabric or cover the walls with either simple or complex patterns. Following the popularity of the hand-painted Chinese papers, English imitations soon followed and were quickly exported to America and France.

Neoclassic and Late Georgian 1750-1810

When it began in Rome and France in the 1740s, the Neoclassic period brought about a revival of classical antiquity that combined the ideals of Europe, Russia, England and America. Borrowing from the simplicity of French Rococo, the Neoclassic period attempted to maintain a renewed return of Renaissance and Baroque ideas so richly embedded in English Rococo. Inspiration also came from the majestic grandeur of Greek and Roman architecture.

Homes made of brick, stone and marble were swirled in a return to classicism. Tones became simpler as bright colors were replaced with pale green, blue, white and gray. Symmetry continues to be a staple of wall paneling as does the combination of a

NEOCLASSIC AND LATE GEORGIAN

21

large panel with two smaller panels. Dadoes were also in fashion but were typically lower than in previous periods. Panel moldings could be painted in contrasting colors or gilded. Mirrors maintained a presence in the home and, much like in the Early Georgian period, could be found on walls and fireplaces, between windows or on furniture. Paneling was commonly adorned with arabesques and classical figures.

By the 1750s, stucco had become a traditional alternative to wood paneling and would often be made to resemble marble, stone or panels. It was during this time too that wallpaper made a surge in demand. Arabesques, architectural papers, textile replicas and Chinese patterns were especially favored. Classical themed tapestries also made a statement in the Neoclassic era.

As the period progressed, Neoclassical ideals soon made their way to England. Blending the concepts of Neo-Palladian with the revival of Greek and Roman art and architecture, Neoclassicism made a statement in Britain and gave new life to the Late Georgian period. Interiors became a true expression of the newly adopted style as stately rooms combined classical design with brightly colored walls, and rugs that complemented a detailed ceiling. Colors became brighter and included lilac, red and vivid pinks, blues and greens, though the middle class maintained the simple color schemes of Early Georgian. Soft

white was preferred for ceilings while imitation marble walls began to make a comeback.

The Neoclassic period put an end to wood paneling that spanned from ceiling to floor. Dadoes remained a consistent presence while the wall above was papered, painted with solid color or adorned with a large mural or several small paintings.

Wallpaper saw an increase in popularity. English, French and Chinese paper took the place of hand-painted details. The styles of paper patterns ranged from Roman columns and molding to landscapes to simple stripes and flowers. Though fabric was still used, it was also replicated with flocked papers, though the imitations were often as costly as the real thing.

Federal, Empire and Regency 1780-1850

Following the end of the American Revolution, leaders of the newly independent nation were looking for a new architectural style. Wealthy Americans continued to build and decorate homes that reflected the Georgian style yet many thought it appropriate to find something different. Meanwhile across the Atlantic, both the Empire and Regency styles were making a name for themselves. The Empire style originated while Emperor Napoleon I ruled the French empire. Regency, a Neoclassical style, fashionable in the United Kingdom, was named for the period from 1811 to 1820, when the Prince of Wales served as regent for Britain's King George III.

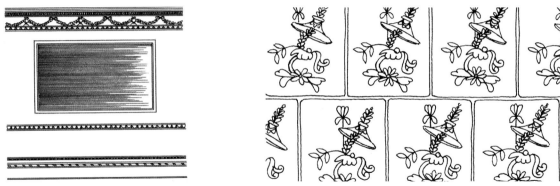

The Federal, Regency and Empire styles became popular in the late 1780s and possessed great similarity to the Neoclassic ideals popular in England and Europe.

The presence of wood paneling continued to lessen as full paneling was out of the question for anything other than a fireplace. Wainscoting was quite favorable yet the wall between the dado and cornice would be simply plastered with a whitewash finish. Carved foliage could often be found on dadoes and pedestals. Paneling could also be painted or grained to give the appearance of rich mahogany. Yet not soon after, wood paneling underwent yet another change and by the 1830s wainscoting had been replaced with strong, grained baseboards.

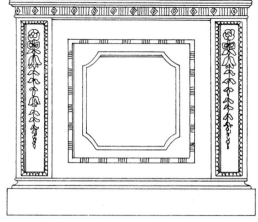

DREAM WALLS

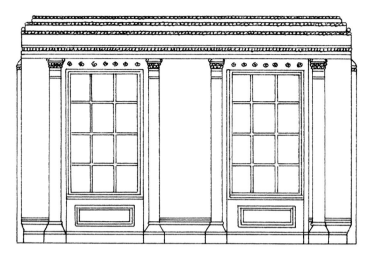

After years of gaining acceptance, the Federal, Regency and Empire styles allowed wallpaper the chance to thrive in the finest rooms of the most opulent homes. Leading up to the 19th century, wallpaper was somewhat plain yet it suddenly took a turn for the sophisticated. In some homes, elaborate borders at the tip of the ceiling, or around wainscoting and doors, could be found.

With the turn of century came bold new patterns of wallpaper. Flowers, stripes, geometric designs and Neoclassical motifs were the new fashion.

French imported scenic wallpaper was prominent in wealthy homes while Greek-influenced wallpaper reflected the revival interests of the period.

As wallpaper and paneling changed, so did painting techniques as walls were coated with brownish red and stone earth tones and deep pinks and grays.

FEDERAL, EMPIRE AND REGENCY

Victorian 1830-1901

Much like an ever-changing modern day America, the Victorian period saw many varying styles during its reign over American design.

As the Victorian era began in the 1830s, critics of the period suggested that a room itself was capable of demanding a specific color. Rooms facing north or east were meant to have warm colors while south or west facing rooms should be cooler. Entryways should be calming, bedrooms and drawing rooms bright and libraries somber. To achieve these varying color tones, the Victorian period encouraged paint, wallpaper and woodwork.

Before the advent of pre-mixed paint, which did not come along until the 1870s, decorators and home owners performed the

task themselves as they attempted to create the pinks, blues, greens, yellows and grays popular in the early decades of the period. With the help of technology, wallpaper became less expensive and more readily available to the general public. The new paper included architectural papers, which imitate panels, cornices, molding, columns and dadoes, landscape papers rich with detail, paper with plants, animals or portraits and papers that gave the illusion of stone or woven fabric. Repeating patterns of stripes, squares or flowers were also quite popular.

Borders became an imperative

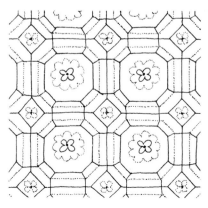

DREAM WALLS

feature of early Victorian design, for a purpose both aesthetic and practical. Borders added a touch of creativity and color yet were also the perfect cover for mistakes and tears.

As the period progressed, design and color became more subtle. With the exception of the dining room, which maintained a preference for rich, deep color, critics began to suggest soft, pastel blues, yellows and greens for the rest of the home. Ivy, oak and maple patterns, both subtle and light in color, were highly recommended. By the 1850s, critics were suggesting actual pine, oak and chestnut be used for wainscoting, though imitation paper still remained quite favorable for both wood and fabric. It was also during this time that chair rails began to make a comeback.

By 1870, America became heavily influenced by an Englishman, Charles Eastlake, who spoke against papering an entire wall, and in favor of wainscoting each room of the home. This followed a widely believed idea that wallpaper was best in moderation. Though few households could afford extensive woodwork throughout the home, the advent of ready-made wainscoting, around 1880, made woodwork less expensive and easy to install. Wallpaper too would often step in to create the appearance of a dado and cornice or frieze. Heavy papers like anaglypta, Japanese leather paper and embossed paper were also gaining popularity.

The final decade of the 19th century saw simplicity in design. No longer would walls be adorned with both wainscoting and a frieze. Dadoes suddenly stepped out of fashion and most existing dadoes were considered to be too high. Wainscoting was limited to halls, dining rooms and libraries.

Myriad materials were still incorporated into design including wallpaper, embossed paper, fabric and paint. Empire wreaths, flowers and patterns that imitated fabric were popular choices in wallpaper. By the end of the 1800s, textured paper became favorable as did alternative concepts that incorporated the designs of Japan and India.

Wallpaper

Like a brilliant chameleon, wallpaper has a way of becoming virtually anything you can imagine.

You can cover the walls with fresh spring flowers, crisp autumn leaves or delicate summer sea shells. You can create the warmth of a Caribbean sunset with soaring green palm trees, soft brown sand and rich red and orange skies. The wonders of the rainforest can come alive with sleek bamboo, lush green wildlife, vibrantly colored Macaws and brilliantly vivid toucans. Or you can transport yourself to the splendor of the Roman era with dramatic columns, noble stone and refined marble.

In the nursery, fluffy yellow ducklings play on multi-colored blocks as they teach a growing mind the ABCs. For little boys and girls, a circus complete with juggling clowns, majestic horses and ferocious lions awaits them as they

DREAM WALLS

DREAM WALLS

rush home from school. And for a young teenager ready to show the world that she's all grown up, there are audacious dragonflies swirling across sleek cream and lavender stripes.

Whether coming into a design as it begins or slipping in at the very end, wallpaper can assume any role that you deem necessary.

As a leader, wallpaper can step into an empty bedroom and create a masterpiece whose canvas gently concludes on the frame of accomplished white wainscoting. From there you will find a soft, rose lampshade and an exquisite, sage quilt that complement the rich colors explored in the wallpaper. In the dining room, wallpaper can take the lead as it covers the walls from ceiling to floor with a Victorian print bold enough to stand alone. The living room can demand striking yet simple furnishings after arriving first with modern textured wallpaper that craves complete attention. And in the kitchen, burgundy wallpaper dressed with knives, forks and spoons stands ready to discover what delicious creations will first be prepared.

Yet wallpaper need not be a leader as it can effortlessly take its place amongst the most complex arrangements of décor. Tranquil yellow can quietly reside within a labyrinth of color. Faded red can add a subtle touch to a bedroom menagerie of beiges, greens and browns. And a vase filled with orchids, tulips and daffodils can inspire a living room to become a living greenhouse that fills your home with the scent of freshly cut flowers. And as it stretches the limits of creativity, there is no room, and no idea that wallpaper cannot be a part of.

DREAM WALLS

DREAM WALLS

DREAM WALLS

WALLPAPER 49

DREAM WALLS

DREAM WALLS

DREAM WALLS

DREAM WALLS

DREAM WALLS

DREAM WALLS

DREAM WALLS

DREAM WALLS

DREAM WALLS

DREAM WALLS

Paint

Step into a room drenched in white and you may not want to stay long. Even with the addition of a brightly colored rug, the walls will continue to call out for something more. More often than not, a touch of paint is all it takes to bring a home to life. As the walls are dressed with color, a room is suddenly given the ability to stir emotion and tantalize the senses.

Take a simple kitchen, add a splash of yellow and instantly you have created a welcome place to begin the day. Whether for a Sunday morning breakfast of strawberries and pancakes or just a quick cup of coffee before work, the bright sun-lit walls will be sure to get you off to an inspiring start.

As for the bathroom, a serene, misty blue can make a

DREAM WALLS

DREAM WALLS

soak in a bubble bath an even more perfect ending to a tiresome day or a mischievous teal can be an inviting playground for a group of rubber duckies waiting for a child's bath time. The effortless addition of paint can take a dining room from merely a place to eat, to a place created to entice your guests with the colors of sparkling champagne, refreshing key lime pie and vanilla bean ice cream infused with boysenberries.

In the living room, a wall immersed in red can evoke stimulating conversation of world events or turn a quiet game of charades into an assembly of award-winning performances.

Perhaps the most interesting possibilities lie in the bedroom, where there is no end to what color can create. There is the tranquil, peaceful environment created by soft browns and greens that welcome you to get lost in a good book. There is the vivacious world of orange and purple that will offer you dynamic energy as you tightly tie your shoes before your first day of high school. And there is the innovative electricity of violet and scarlet that will whirl your imagination as you prepare to compose your next screenplay.

In the rooms of younger children, color can captivate their dreams of enchantment. Vivid reds and yellows can take a little boy on a wild adventure while rose and lavender can make a little girl feel like princess. Or, for

DREAM WALLS

something truly special, a child's room can become a world of wonder when paint transforms their simple walls into their favorite Saturday morning cartoon.

For the nursery, along with pink for girls and blue for boys, soft chartreuse and murmured white can gently welcome a new life into your home.

But no matter what shades you choose, and no matter where in your home you explore the possibilities of color, paint will always tempt your senses as it strives to make your house a home.

DREAM WALLS

DREAM WALLS

DREAM WALLS

DREAM WALLS

DREAM WALLS

DREAM WALLS

DREAM WALLS

DREAM WALLS

DREAM WALLS

DREAM WALLS

Stone and Tile

As you look around your home, chances are stone and tile are part of your decorative style. There are small pink squares of shower tile you casually glance at while giving the family dog a bath. There are rocks and pebbles amongst the yellow and white daffodils that stand in the front garden. And there are remnants of a powder blue floor tile hiding beneath the kitchen rug. But contemporary stone and tile can be so much more than you expect.

From Bluffstone to Country Rubble, from River Rock to Stacked Stone, modern stone has taken on new colors and new shapes and has become a fresh decorating choice. And as it delves into new possibilities, modern

stone is not without its tradition. There will always be something so warm and inviting about a stone fireplace and now this architectural staple has made its way into each room of the home. As you sit reading by the fire on a brisk winter night, you may do so in front of a stone creation that reaches to the bedroom ceiling. Or perhaps a dinner with friends can be warmed with a dining room fireplace.

Yet modern stone need not stop there. It can be interspersed with French doors to create an inviting pathway from your home to the cool blue water of your swimming pool. It can bring strength to a hallway or creativity to a stairway. And as it steps into the future, stone can also bring with it a whisper of the past as it turns a simple basement into a 18th-century wine cellar filled with rich red merlots and spicy scarlet cabernets.

Though traditionally more prominent that stone, tile too has taken on a modern and refreshing approach to contemporary decorating. Still a staple of bathrooms and kitchens, modern tile explores creativity with imaginative magnificence. Colors, patterns, shapes and textures are stretching the limits and discovering endless possibilities.

DREAM WALLS

DREAM WALLS

In the master bathroom, vanilla cream tile can create small steps that lead to a sunken white bathtub swirling amongst soft cocoa walls. Downstairs, a tiled patchwork quilt is created to reflect the vivid colors of the flowers that sit in the window sill. And in the kitchen, mystic green, hazelnut brown and custard white come together to create a mosaic wonder that transforms simple walls into a stunning display of artistic talent. Much like stone, tile is also appearing in many unexpected places whether it finds itself establishing a solarium rich with plants, sparking afternoon conversation in the living room or climbing to the ceiling to create a midnight blue and dusty beige fireplace. And with the new directions design is continuing to pursue, there is no telling where modern stone and tile may turn up next.

DREAM WALLS

DREAM WALLS

DREAM WALLS

DREAM WALLS

DREAM WALLS

Dream Walls

DREAM WALLS

DREAM WALLS

Wood Paneling

With its roots deep in American history, wood paneling is as much a part of America's heritage as George Washington and apple pie. Yet before coming across the Atlantic, wood paneling made an impression in some of the most opulent homes of Renaissance and Baroque Europe.

As a combination of Early American and Classic European, modern wood paneling brings an heir of distinction and elegance to contemporary walls.

Though it appears limited by form and color, wood paneling is perhaps more versatile than you would imagine. Myriad combinations can be created when the styles of recessed, raised and beadboard wood paneling are blended with the colors of oak, maple and mahogany. And wood paneling need not be afraid to embrace white, cream and splashes of color.

The bedroom can be adorned with brilliant white recessed panels that span from the plush caramel carpet to the center of the fresh peach walls. If rich hardwood floors help to create your perfect bedroom, complement the colors with a blanket of coral that flawlessly combines wall and paneling.

In the study, raised panels of deep oak converge with a book shelf filled with the works of William Shakespeare and Edgar Allen Poe while cream,

DREAM WALLS

raised wood paneling frames a living room window that looks out to a field of blossoming red apple trees. Beadboard, with its slim, sleek design, can traverse a rich blue wall to bridge white wainscoting and wooden ceiling trim as you gaze into the bathroom mirror, preparing for a spectacular night at the opera. Or a dining room rich with pink and white muraled wallpaper can be gently laced with narrow beadboard that sits below a stretch of bright fuchsia trim. And once you have invited wood paneling into your home, there is no end to the warmth and subtle elegance it will provide.

DREAM WALLS

DREAM WALLS

DREAM WALLS

DREAM WALLS

DREAM WALLS

WOOD PANELING

DREAM WALLS

DREAM WALLS

DREAM WALLS

DREAM WALLS

WOOD PANELING

DREAM WALLS

DREAM WALLS

DREAM WALLS

Alternative Wall Coverings

Beyond the endless potential of wallpaper, paint, stone, tile and wood paneling you will find an elaborate array of innovative room concepts that lie waiting to be discovered.

An undersea world of exotic fish and vibrantly colored coral can come to life in your home as a built-in aquarium is interspersed with rich maple paneling.

The combination of a rich rusted wall and a dramatic wooden sculpture can turn a modest living room into a striking art gallery. Sometimes, a wall need not be a wall at all as modern architecture takes over and creates dynamic arches and entryways. With the delicate detail of a tiered wedding cake, wall flowering turns shy walls into a breathless canvas waiting to be adorned with swirls of flowers.

Rustic log walls will effortlessly transport your home to the good old days of quiet, country living and to travel deeper into the past, walls can be dressed with fabric and tapestries that remember an era of opulence and grandeur.

DREAM WALLS

Quite effortlessly, creativity can be conjured when a precisely placed armoire or hutch is surrounded by modern lighting that gently hangs nearby.

With daring imagination, murals can suppose an ivy-covered atrium that looks out to crystal blue lake or a pair of sparrows taking flight amongst a cluster of clouds. Brick can be warmed with a splash of sunshine yellow or deep chestnut while a faux finish can allow a foyer to become a 14th century castle or an ancient marbled cathedral. If looking for the purity of Asian design, sliding screen walls made of translucent paper and delicate lattice woodwork can evoke the innocence of a Japanese tea house.

Texture and color can combine to captivate attention as cream colored walls are brightened with vivid and unique works of art.

When modern is not modern enough, plasma televisions and cinematic screens can at once be the focal point of a room while they dissolve into the decor.

Eclectic fusion allows for the blending of form and flexibility while it balances the many instruments of design. So whether you expand on tradition or escape it entirely, fearless innovation is all you need to create a wall that is uniquely yours. And with the dynamic parade of choices that await you, there is no limit to what you may create.

DREAM WALLS

ALTERNATIVE WALL COVERINGS: RUSTIC LOG WALLS

DREAM WALLS

DREAM WALLS

DREAM WALLS

Dream Walls

ALTERNATIVE WALL COVERINGS: BRICK AND FAUX FINISH

DREAM WALLS

DREAM WALLS

DREAM WALLS

ALTERNATIVE WALL COVERINGS: FAUX FINISH

DREAM WALLS

DREAM WALLS

DREAM WALLS

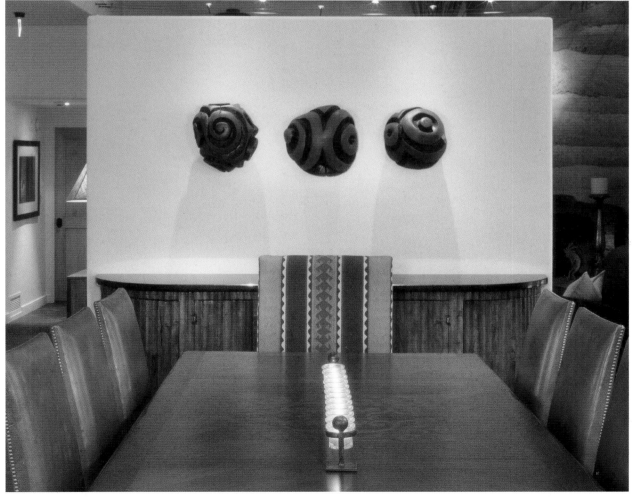

DREAM WALLS

DREAM WALLS

DREAM WALLS

DREAM WALLS

DREAM WALLS

DREAM WALLS

DREAM WALLS

234

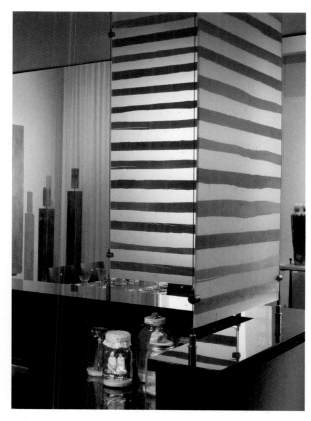

DREAM WALLS

DREAM WALLS

DREAM WALLS

DREAM WALLS

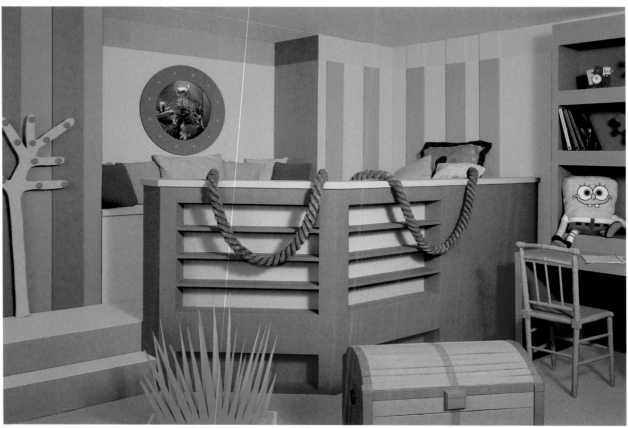

246

DREAM WALLS

252

DREAM WALLS

DREAM WALLS

DREAM WALLS

DREAM WALLS

DREAM WALLS

Wallpaper Catalog

Page 32	**Page 33a**	**Page 33b**	**Page 33c**	**Page 33d**
Seabrook QC3527X	Seabrook BU11454B	Seabrook BU11504	Seabrook BU12607	Seabrook BU11107
Page 33e	**Page 34a**	**Page 34b**	**Page 34c**	**Page 34d**
Seabrook BS20407	Seabrook US20901	Seabrook US20851B	Seabrook US21001	Seabrook GG31857B
Page 34e	**Page 35a**	**Page 35b**	**Page 36a**	**Page 36b**
Seabrook GG32007	Seabrook US20103	Seabrook NP1871	Seabrook TV2718	Seabrook HV6552
Page 37a	**Page 37b**	**Page 37c**	**Page 37d**	**Page 38**
Seabrook NP1894	Seabrook HG582	Seabrook HG531B	Seabrook ET288X	Seabrook BM70509
Page 39a	**Page 39b**	**Page 40a**	**Page 40b**	**Page 40c**
Seabrook HU6189	Seabrook SC51405	Seabrook BS22359B	Seabrook BS20509	Seabrook BS22209

Page 41a

Seabrook
BU13508

Page 41b

Seabrook
BL22318BX

Page 42a

Seabrook
PP361

Page 42b

Seabrook
PP358B

Page 43a

Seabrook
PP301B

Page 43b

Seabrook
PP305

Page 43c

Seabrook
PP308

Page 43d

Seabrook
PP402

Page 43e

Seabrook
PP400B

Page 43f

Seabrook
PP394

Page 44a

Seabrook
BU13003

Page 44b

Seabrook
BU10303

Page 44c

Seabrook
BS20407

Page 44d

Seabrook
BS20207

Page 45a

Seabrook
GG33101

Page 45b

Seabrook
GG31601

Page 46

Seabrook
AH21721

Page 47a

Seabrook
SC52910

Page 47b

Seabrook
HU6134

Page 48a

Seabrook
SC52804

Page 48b

Seabrook
TV2824

Page 48c

Seabrook
TV2832

Page 49a

Seabrook
NP1979

Page 49b

Seabrook
NP1832

Page 49c

Seabrook
NP1920

DREAM WALLS

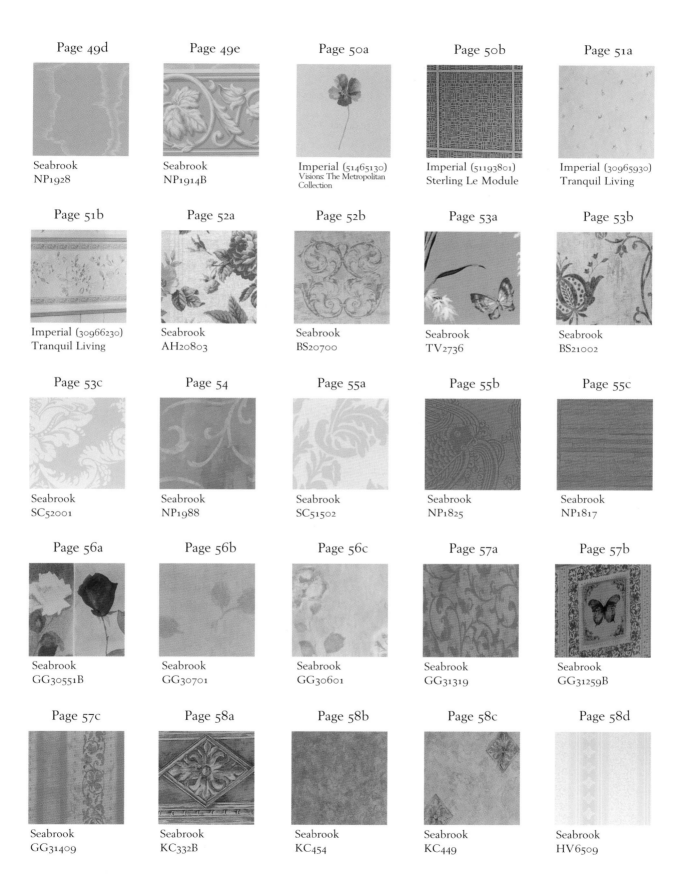

Page 49d
Seabrook
NP1928

Page 49e
Seabrook
NP1914B

Page 50a
Imperial (51465130)
Visions: The Metropolitan
Collection

Page 50b
Imperial (51193801)
Sterling Le Module

Page 51a
Imperial (30965930)
Tranquil Living

Page 51b
Imperial (30966230)
Tranquil Living

Page 52a
Seabrook
AH20803

Page 52b
Seabrook
BS20700

Page 53a
Seabrook
TV2736

Page 53b
Seabrook
BS21002

Page 53c
Seabrook
SC52001

Page 54
Seabrook
NP1988

Page 55a
Seabrook
SC51502

Page 55b
Seabrook
NP1825

Page 55c
Seabrook
NP1817

Page 56a
Seabrook
GG30551B

Page 56b
Seabrook
GG30701

Page 56c
Seabrook
GG30601

Page 57a
Seabrook
GG31319

Page 57b
Seabrook
GG31259B

Page 57c
Seabrook
GG31409

Page 58a
Seabrook
KC332B

Page 58b
Seabrook
KC454

Page 58c
Seabrook
KC449

Page 58d
Seabrook
HV6509

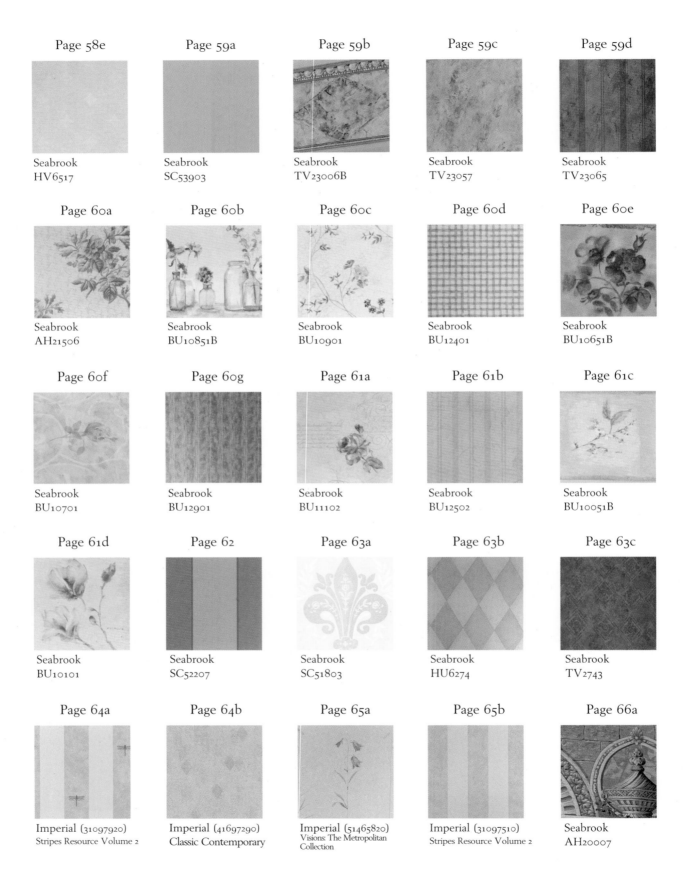

Page 58e

Seabrook
HV6517

Page 59a

Seabrook
SC53903

Page 59b

Seabrook
TV23006B

Page 59c

Seabrook
TV23057

Page 59d

Seabrook
TV23065

Page 60a

Seabrook
AH21506

Page 60b

Seabrook
BU10851B

Page 60c

Seabrook
BU10901

Page 60d

Seabrook
BU12401

Page 60e

Seabrook
BU10651B

Page 60f

Seabrook
BU10701

Page 60g

Seabrook
BU12901

Page 61a

Seabrook
BU11102

Page 61b

Seabrook
BU12502

Page 61c

Seabrook
BU10051B

Page 61d

Seabrook
BU10101

Page 62

Seabrook
SC52207

Page 63a

Seabrook
SC51803

Page 63b

Seabrook
HU6274

Page 63c

Seabrook
TV2743

Page 64a

Imperial (31097920)
Stripes Resource Volume 2

Page 64b

Imperial (41697290)
Classic Contemporary

Page 65a

Imperial (51465820)
Visions: The Metropolitan
Collection

Page 65b

Imperial (31097510)
Stripes Resource Volume 2

Page 66a

Seabrook
AH20007

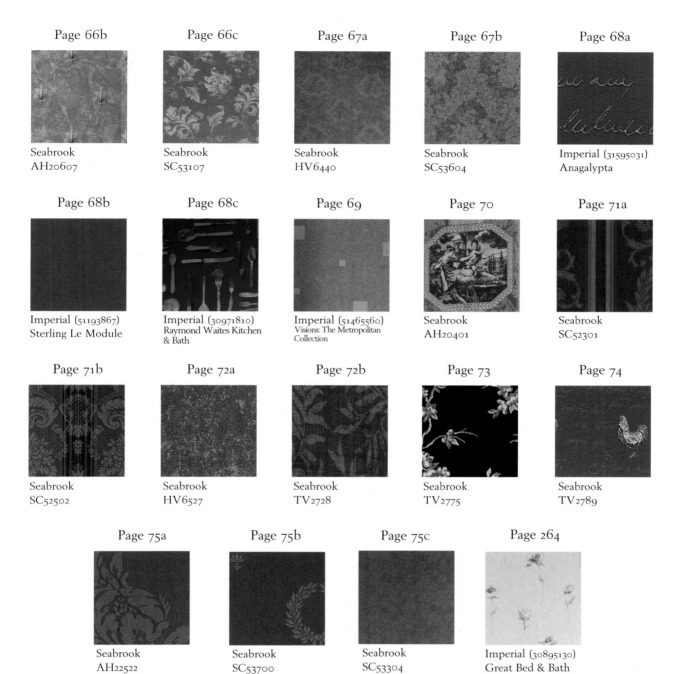

Page 66b	Page 66c	Page 67a	Page 67b	Page 68a
Seabrook AH20607	Seabrook SC53107	Seabrook HV6440	Seabrook SC53604	Imperial (31595031) Anagalypta
Page 68b	Page 68c	Page 69	Page 70	Page 71a
Imperial (51193867) Sterling Le Module	Imperial (30971810) Raymond Waites Kitchen & Bath	Imperial (51465560) Visions: The Metropolitan Collection	Seabrook AH20401	Seabrook SC52301
Page 71b	Page 72a	Page 72b	Page 73	Page 74
Seabrook SC52502	Seabrook HV6527	Seabrook TV2728	Seabrook TV2775	Seabrook TV2789
Page 75a	Page 75b	Page 75c	Page 264	
Seabrook AH22522	Seabrook SC53700	Seabrook SC53304	Imperial (30895130) Great Bed & Bath	

Paint Catalog

Page 76	Page 76	Page 77 (top)	Page 77 (bottom)	Page 78 (top)
Glidden Wildflower Wind	Glidden Pure White Semi-Gloss	Valspar Porcelain Red	Valspar Waverly Willow	Valspar Dusky Purple
Page 78 (top)	Page 78 (bottom)	Page 78 (bottom)	Page 78 (bottom)	Page 78 (bottom)
Valspar Violet Sweet	Valspar Pink Odyssey	Valspar Sassy Lilac	Valspar Warm Pink	Valspar Sweet Pink
Page 78 (bottom)	Page 78 (bottom)	Page 78 (bottom)	Page 78 (bottom)	Page 79 (top)
Valspar Hushed Rose	Valspar Purple Whisper	Valspar Iris Moon	Valspar Gentle Wind	Valspar Positively Purple
Page 79 (top)	Page 79 (top)	Page 79 (top)	Page 79 (top)	Page 79 (bottom)
Valspar Cosmic Berry	Valspar Purple Royalty	Valspar Karmic Grape	Valspar Berries Galore	Valspar Dusty Lavender
Page 79 (bottom)	Page 80 (top)	Page 80 (top)	Page 80 (bottom)	Page 81 (top left)
Valspar Lilac Intuition	Glidden Surfside	Glidden Pure White Gloss	Valspar Powder Blue 4	Valspar Granite Sea Agate

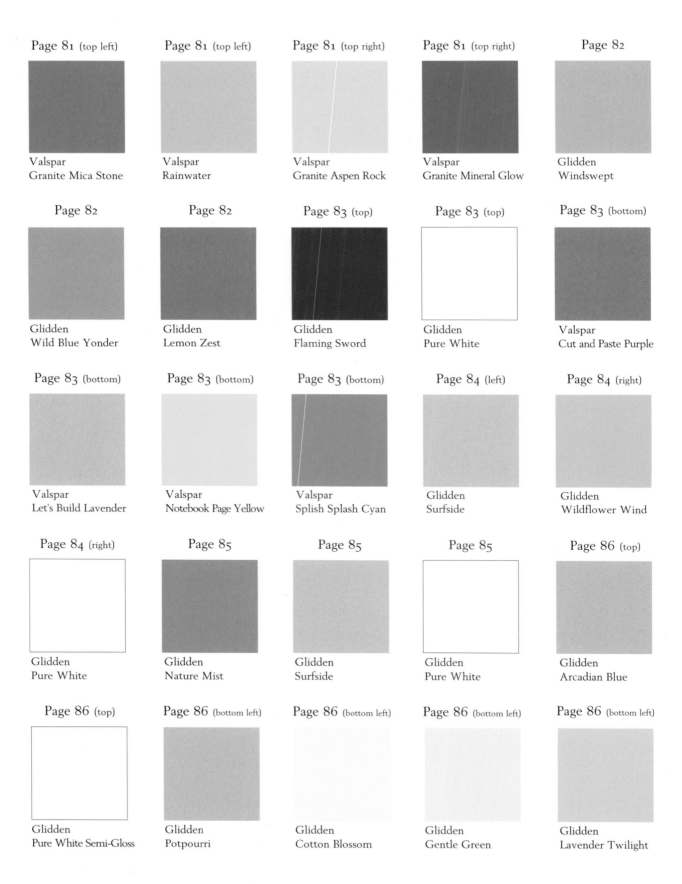

Page 81 (top left)

Valspar
Granite Mica Stone

Page 81 (top left)

Valspar
Rainwater

Page 81 (top right)

Valspar
Granite Aspen Rock

Page 81 (top right)

Valspar
Granite Mineral Glow

Page 82

Glidden
Windswept

Page 82

Glidden
Wild Blue Yonder

Page 82

Glidden
Lemon Zest

Page 83 (top)

Glidden
Flaming Sword

Page 83 (top)

Glidden
Pure White

Page 83 (bottom)

Valspar
Cut and Paste Purple

Page 83 (bottom)

Valspar
Let's Build Lavender

Page 83 (bottom)

Valspar
Notebook Page Yellow

Page 83 (bottom)

Valspar
Splish Splash Cyan

Page 84 (left)

Glidden
Surfside

Page 84 (right)

Glidden
Wildflower Wind

Page 84 (right)

Glidden
Pure White

Page 85

Glidden
Nature Mist

Page 85

Glidden
Surfside

Page 85

Glidden
Pure White

Page 86 (top)

Glidden
Arcadian Blue

Page 86 (top)

Glidden
Pure White Semi-Gloss

Page 86 (bottom left)

Glidden
Potpourri

Page 86 (bottom left)

Glidden
Cotton Blossom

Page 86 (bottom left)

Glidden
Gentle Green

Page 86 (bottom left)

Glidden
Lavender Twilight

DREAM WALLS

Page 86 (bottom right)

Glidden
Arcadian Blue

Page 86 (bottom right)

Glidden
Pure White Semi-Gloss

Page 87 (top)

Glidden
Carnation Pink

Page 87 (top)

Glidden
Pure White Semi-Gloss

Page 87 (bottom)

Glidden
Skyline

Page 88 & 89

Glidden
Newborn (Wall)

Page 88 & 89

Glidden
Jonquil (Stencil)

Page 88 & 89

Glidden
Sun Rays (Stencil)

Page 88 & 89

Glidden
Dandelion (Stencil)

Page 88 & 89

Glidden
Pure White (Trim)

Page 90 (top left)

Glidden
Carotene

Page 90 (top right)

Glidden
Blue Silk

Page 90 (top right)

Glidden
Nostalgic

Page 90 (top right)

Glidden
Encore

Page 90 (bottom)

Glidden
Forest Floor

Page 90 (bottom)

Glidden
Khaki Sun

Page 91 (top)

Glidden
Flaming Sword

Page 91 (top)

Glidden
Rapture

Page 91 (bottom)

Glidden
Prelude Blue

Page 92

Glidden
Crisp Linen

Page 92

Glidden
Calm Sea

Page 92

Glidden
Seaside Village

Page 92

Glidden
Stowe White

Page 93 (top & bottom left)

Glidden
European White

Page 93 (top & bottom left)

Glidden
Pure White

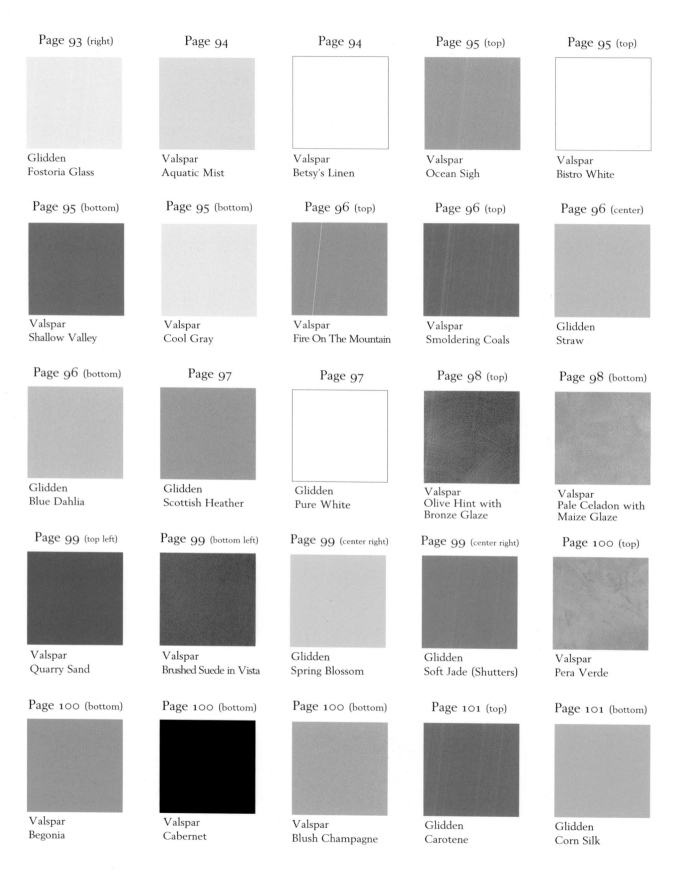

Page 93 (right)
Glidden
Fostoria Glass

Page 94
Valspar
Aquatic Mist

Page 94
Valspar
Betsy's Linen

Page 95 (top)
Valspar
Ocean Sigh

Page 95 (top)
Valspar
Bistro White

Page 95 (bottom)
Valspar
Shallow Valley

Page 95 (bottom)
Valspar
Cool Gray

Page 96 (top)
Valspar
Fire On The Mountain

Page 96 (top)
Valspar
Smoldering Coals

Page 96 (center)
Glidden
Straw

Page 96 (bottom)
Glidden
Blue Dahlia

Page 97
Glidden
Scottish Heather

Page 97
Glidden
Pure White

Page 98 (top)
Valspar
Olive Hint with
Bronze Glaze

Page 98 (bottom)
Valspar
Pale Celadon with
Maize Glaze

Page 99 (top left)
Valspar
Quarry Sand

Page 99 (bottom left)
Valspar
Brushed Suede in Vista

Page 99 (center right)
Glidden
Spring Blossom

Page 99 (center right)
Glidden
Soft Jade (Shutters)

Page 100 (top)
Valspar
Pera Verde

Page 100 (bottom)
Valspar
Begonia

Page 100 (bottom)
Valspar
Cabernet

Page 100 (bottom)
Valspar
Blush Champagne

Page 101 (top)
Glidden
Carotene

Page 101 (bottom)
Glidden
Corn Silk

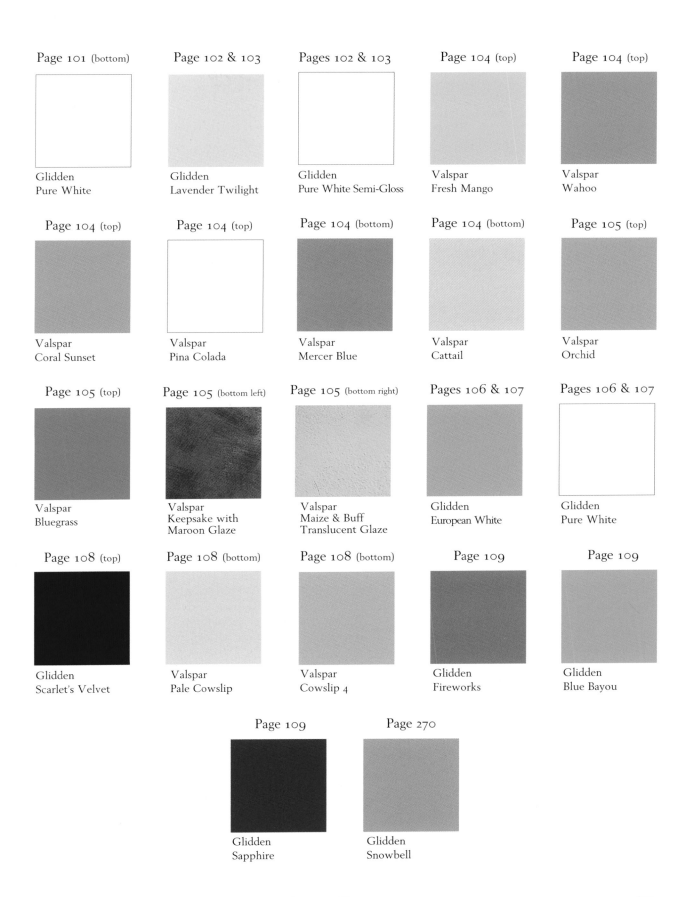

Page 101 (bottom)

Glidden
Pure White

Page 102 & 103

Glidden
Lavender Twilight

Pages 102 & 103

Glidden
Pure White Semi-Gloss

Page 104 (top)

Valspar
Fresh Mango

Page 104 (top)

Valspar
Wahoo

Page 104 (top)

Valspar
Coral Sunset

Page 104 (top)

Valspar
Pina Colada

Page 104 (bottom)

Valspar
Mercer Blue

Page 104 (bottom)

Valspar
Cattail

Page 105 (top)

Valspar
Orchid

Page 105 (top)

Valspar
Bluegrass

Page 105 (bottom left)

Valspar
Keepsake with
Maroon Glaze

Page 105 (bottom right)

Valspar
Maize & Buff
Translucent Glaze

Pages 106 & 107

Glidden
European White

Pages 106 & 107

Glidden
Pure White

Page 108 (top)

Glidden
Scarlet's Velvet

Page 108 (bottom)

Valspar
Pale Cowslip

Page 108 (bottom)

Valspar
Cowslip 4

Page 109

Glidden
Fireworks

Page 109

Glidden
Blue Bayou

Page 109

Glidden
Sapphire

Page 270

Glidden
Snowbell

Page 1
Design created by Kari Whitman Interiors; 310-652-8684; www.kariwhitmaninteriors.com

Pages 2-3
Design created by Kari Whitman Interiors; 310-652-8684; www.kariwhitmaninteriors.com

Pages 6-7
Design created by Imperial Home Décor Group; 888-608-5943; www.ihdg.com

Pages 32-75 (see wallpaper catalog)
Seabrook Wallcoverings; 800-238-9152; www.seabrookwallcoverings.com; Imperial Home Décor Group; 888-608-5943; www.ihdg.com

Pages 76-109 (see paint catalog)
Glidden, an ICI Paints brand; 800-GLIDDEN; www.glidden.com Valspar; 800-845-9061; www.valspar.com

Page 110
Design created by Leslie Harris Interior Design; 323-651-1422; www.leslieharrisinteriors.com

Page 111
Top: Design created by Richens Designs, Inc.; 310 385-8450; www.richensdesigns.com Bottom: Design created by El Dorado Stone; 800-925-1491; www.eldoradostone.com

Page 112
Top: Design created by Florida Tile; 800-789-TILE; www.floridatile.com Bottom left/right: Design created by Dal-Tile; 214-398-1411; www.daltile.com

Page 113
Design created by Dal-Tile; 214-398-1411; www.daltile.com

Page 114
Design created by Richens Designs, Inc.; 310 385-8450; www.richensdesigns.com

Page 115
Top right: Design created by El Dorado Stone; 800-925-1491; www.eldoradostone.com Bottom right: Design created by Cultured Stone Corp.;

800-255-1727; www.culturedstone.com

Page 116
Design created by Florida Tile; 800-789-TILE; www.floridatile.com

Page 117
Top/Bottom: Design created by Florida Tile; 800-789-TILE; www.floridatile.com

Page 118
Design created by Cultured Stone Corp.; 800-255-1727; www.culturedstone.com

Page 119
All: Design created by Cultured Stone Corp.; 800-255-1727; www.culturedstone.com

Page 120
All: Design created by Dal-Tile; 214-398-1411; www.daltile.com

Page 121
Design created by Florida Tile; 800-789-TILE; www.floridatile.com

Page 122
Top/Bottom: Design created by Lori Carroll; 520-886-3443; www.loricarroll.com

Page 123
Design created by Lori Carroll; 520-886-3443; www.loricarroll.com

Page 124
All: Design created by Dal-Tile; 214-398-1411; www.daltile.com

Page 125
Left/Top Right: Design created by Dal-Tile; 214-398-1411; www.daltile.com Center right/Bottom right: Design created by Florida Tile; 800-789-TILE; www.floridatile.com

Page 126
Design created by Cultured Stone Corp.; 800-255-1727; www.culturedstone.com

Page 127
Top left/Bottom: Design created by Cultured Stone Corp.; 800-255-1727; www.culturedstone.com

Top right: Design created by Lori Carroll; 520-886-3443; www.loricarroll.com

Page 128
Design created by Florida Tile; 800-789-TILE; www.floridatile.com

Page 129
Top right/Bottom right: Design created by Florida Tile; 800-789-TILE; www.floridatile.com

Page 130
Design created by Dal-Tile; 214-398-1411; www.daltile.com

Page 131
Top: Design created by Cultured Stone Corp.; 800-255-1727; www.culturedstone.com Bottom: Design created by El Dorado Stone; 800-925-1491; www.eldoradostone.com

Page 132
Top left/Bottom left: Design created by Florida Tile; 800-789-TILE; www.floridatile.com Center: Design created by Dal-Tile; 214-398-1411; www.daltile.com

Page 133
Top/Bottom: Design created by Dal-Tile; 214-398-1411; www.daltile.com

Page 134
Top: Design created by El Dorado Stone; 800-925-1491; www.eldoradostone.com Bottom: Design created by Cultured Stone Corp.; 800-255-1727; www.culturedstone.com

Page 135
Design created by Cultured Stone Corp.; 800-255-1727; www.culturedstone.com

Page 136
Top: Design created by Dal-Tile; 214-398-1411; www.daltile.com Bottom: Design created by Florida Tile; 800-789-TILE; www.floridatile.com

Page 137
Top/Bottom: Design created by Florida Tile; 800-789-TILE; www.floridatile.com

Page 138
Top: Design created by El Dorado Stone; 800-925-1491; www.eldoradostone.com Bottom: Design created by Cultured Stone Corp.; 800-255-1727; www.culturedstone.com

Page 139
Top/Bottom: Design created by Cultured Stone Corp.; 800-255-1727; www.culturedstone.com

Page 140
Design created by Bonnie Sachs; 310-306-4595; www.bonniesachs.com

Page 141
Top/Bottom: Design created by Dal-Tile; 214-398-1411; www.daltile.com

Page 142
Design created by New England Classic; 888-880-6324; www.newenglandclassic.com

Page 143
Top: Design created by New England Classic; 888-880-6324; www.newenglandclassic.com Bottom: Design created by Imperial Home Décor Group; 888-608-5943; www. ihdg.com

Page 144
All: Design created by New England Classic; 888-880-6324; www.newenglandclassic.com

Page 145
Design created by Lori Carroll & Associates; 520-886-3443; www.loricarroll.com

Page 146
Design created by New England Classic; 888-880-6324; www.newenglandclassic.com

Page 147
Design created by New England Classic; 888-880-6324; www.newenglandclassic.com

Page 148
Top/Bottom: Design created by Cheryl Gardner Interior Design; 323-856-0812; www.cherylgardner.com

Page 149
Design created by Cheryl Gardner Interior Design;

323-856-0812;
www.cherylgardner.com

Page 150
Design created by Richens Designs, Inc.; 310 385-8450; www.richensdesigns.com

Page 151
Top/Bottom: Design created by New England Classic; 888-880-6324; www.newenglandclassic.com

Page 152
All: Design created by New England Classic; 888-880-6324; www.newenglandclassic.com

Page 153
All: Design created by New England Classic; 888-880-6324; www.newenglandclassic.com

Page 154
Design created by New England Classic; 888-880-6324; www.newenglandclassic.com

Page 155
Top/Bottom: Design created by New England Classic; 888-880-6324; www.newenglandclassic.com

Pages 156-157
Design created by New England Classic; 888-880-6324; www.newenglandclassic.com

Page 158
Design created by New England Classic; 888-880-6324; www.newenglandclassic.com

Page 159
Top/Bottom: Design created by New England Classic; 888-880-6324; www.newenglandclassic.com

Page 160
Top/Bottom: Design created by New England Classic; 888-880-6324; www.newenglandclassic.com

Page 161
Design created by Leslie Harris Interior Design; 323-651-1422; www.leslieharrisinteriors.com

Page 162
Design created by New England Classic; 888-880-6324; www.newenglandclassic.com

Page 163
Top: Design created by Stroheim & Romann; 718-706-7000; www.stroheim.com

Bottom: Design created by New England Classic; 888-880-6324; www.newenglandclassic.com

Page 164
Design created by Valspar; 800-845-9061; www.valspar.com

Page 165
Top/Bottom: Design created by Valspar; 800-845-9061; www.valspar.com

Page 166
Top/Bottom: Design created by New England Classic; 888-880-6324; www.newenglandclassic.com

Page 167
Design created by New England Classic; 888-880-6324; www.newenglandclassic.com

Page 168
Design created by Richens Designs, Inc.; 310 385-8450; www.richensdesigns.com

Page 169
Top: Design created by Rink Reynolds Diamond Fisher Wilson PA; 904-396-6353; www.rrdfw.com

Bottom: Design created by New England Classic; 888-880-6324; www.newenglandclassic.com

Page 170
Top: Design courtesy of the Randall family

Bottom: Design created by New England Classic; 888-880-6324; www.newenglandclassic.com

Page 171
Top: Design created by New England Classic; 888-880-6324; www.newenglandclassic.com

Bottom: Design courtesy of the Randall family

Page 172
Top: Design created by German Sonntag; 310-452-2757

Bottom: Design created by Rink Reynolds Diamond Fisher Wilson PA; 904-396-6353; www.rrdfw.com

Page 173
Design created by German Sonntag; 310-452-2757

Page 174
Design created by Glidden, an ICI Paints brand;

800-GLIDDEN; www.glidden.com

Page 175
Top: Design created by Imperial Home Décor Group; 888-608-5943; www.ihdg.com

Bottom: Design created by New England Classic; 888-880-6324; www.newenglandclassic.com

Page 176
Design created by Lori Carroll & Associates; 520-886-3443; www.loricarroll.com

Page 177
Top left: Design created by Age of Aquariums; 562-438-6252

Bottom left: Design created by Rink Reynolds Diamond Fisher Wilson PA; 904-396-6353; www.rrdfw.com

Top right: Design created by Lori Carroll & Associates; 520-886-3443; www.loricarroll.com

Page 178
Design created by Richens Designs, Inc.; 310 385-8450; www.richensdesigns.com

Page 179
Top: Design created by Leslie Harris Interior Design; 323-651-1422; www.leslieharrisinteriors.com

Bottom: Design created by Cheryl Gardner Interior Design; 323-856-0812; www.cherylgardner.com

Page 180-181
Design created by Zdravko Terziev; 415-924-5147; www.wallflowering.com

Page 182
Top: Design created by Rim Rock's Dogwood Cabins; 618-264-6036; www.rimrocksdogwoodcabins.com

Bottom: Design created by AmerLink: 800-872-4254; www.amerlink.com

Page 183
Design created by AmerLink: 800-872-4254; www.amerlink.com

Pages 184-185
All: Design created by Stroheim & Romann, Inc; 718-706-7000;

www.stroheim.com

Pages 186-187
All: Design created by Lori Carroll & Associates; 520-886-3443; www.loricarroll.com

Page 188
Design created by 4walls.com; 800-496-4444; www.4walls.com

Page 189
Top/Bottom right: Design created by Seabrook Wallcoverings; 800-238-9152; www.seabrookwallcoverings.com

Bottom left: Design created by Imperial Home Décor Group; 888-608-5943; www.ihdg.com

Page 190
Both: Design created by Valspar; 800-845-9061; www.valspar.com

Page 191
Design created by Kari Whitman Interiors; 310-652-8684; www.kariwhitmaninteriors.com

Page 192
Design created by Boyce Products Ltd; 212-683-3100; www.boyceproducts.com

Page 193
All: Designs created by Interior Spaces, Inc; 310-399-4033; www.interiorspacesinc.com

Pages 194-195
All: Design created by Lori Carroll & Associates; 520-886-3443; www.loricarroll.com

Page 196
Top: Design created by Bonnie Sachs; 310-306-4595; www.bonniesachs.com

Bottom (both): Design created by Richens Designs, Inc.; 310 385-8450; www.richensdesigns.com

Page 197
Design created by Lori Carroll & Associates; 520-886-3443; www.loricarroll.com

Page 198
Top left: Design created by Leslie Harris Interior Design; 323-651-1422; www.leslieharrisinteriors.com

Top right/Bottom left/right: Design created by Lori Carroll & Associates; 520-886-3443; www.loricarroll.com

Page 199
All: Design created by Lori Carroll & Associates; 520-886-3443; www.loricarroll.com

Page 200
Design created by Leslie Harris Interior Design; 323-651-1422; www.leslieharrisinteriors.com

Page 201
Top: Design created by Lori Carroll & Associates; 520-886-3443; www.loricarroll.com Bottom: Design created by Leslie Harris Interior Design; 323-651-1422; www.leslieharrisinteriors.com

Page 202
Top/Bottom: Design created by 4walls.com; 800-496-4444; www.4walls.com

Page 203
Design created by Seabrook Wallcoverings; 800-238-9152; www.seabrookwallcoverings.com

Pages 204-205
All: Design created by The Cheesecake Factory; www.cheesecakefactory.com

Pages 206-207
All: Design created by Zdravko Terziev; 415-924-5147; www.wallflowering.com

Page 208
Design created by Lori Carroll & Associates; 520-886-3443; www.loricarroll.com

Page 209
Top/Center: Design created by BNK Design Consultants; 610-941-2943; www.BNKdesign.com Bottom left: Design created by Architectural Masterworks; 510-486-8778; www.newarigallery.com

Pages 210-211
Design created by Lori Carroll & Associates; 520-886-3443; www.loricarroll.com

Page 212
Design created by Lori Carroll & Associates; 520-886-3443; www.loricarroll.com

Page 213
Top: Design created by Leslie Harris Interior Design; 323-651-1422; www.leslieharrisinteriors.com Bottom: Design created by Lori Carroll & Associates; 520-886-3443; www.loricarroll.com

Pages 214-215
All: Design created by Imperial Home Décor Group; 888-608-5943; www.ihdg.com

Pages 216-217
All: Design created by Valspar; 800-845-9061; www.valspar.com

Page 218
Top left: Design created by Glidden, an ICI Paints brand; 800-GLIDDEN; www.glidden.com Top right/Bottom left/right: Design created by Valspar; 800-845-9061; www.valspar.com

Page 219
Top left/right/Bottom right: Design created by Valspar; 800-845-9061; www.valspar.com Bottom left: Design created by Glidden, an ICI Paints brand; 800-GLIDDEN; www.glidden.com

Page 220
Top/Bottom left/right: Design created by Imperial Home Décor Group; 888-608-5943; www.ihdg.com Bottom center: Design created by Seabrook Wallcoverings; 800-238-9152; www.seabrookwallcoverings.com

Page 221
Top left/Top right/Center right: Design created by Imperial Home Décor Group; 888-608-5943; www.ihdg.com Bottom right: Design created by Seabrook Wallcoverings; 800-238-9152; www.seabrookwallcoverings.com

Page 222
Top: Design created by Leslie Harris Interior Design; 323-651-1422; www.leslieharrisinteriors.com Bottom left: Design created by El Dorado Stone; 800-925-1491; www.eldoradostone.com Bottom right: Design created

by Cultured Stone Corp.; 800-255-1727; www.culturedstone.com

Page 223
Top left/right/Bottom right: Design created by Cultured Stone Corp.; 800-255-1727; www.culturedstone.com Bottom left: Design created by El Dorado Stone; 800-925-1491; www.eldoradostone.com

Page 224
All: Design created by Seabrook Wallcoverings; 800-238-9152; www.seabrookwallcoverings.com

Page 225
Top left/Bottom right: Design created by Imperial Home Décor Group; 888-608-5943; www.ihdg.com Top right: Design created by Seabrook Wallcoverings; 800-238-9152; www.seabrookwallcoverings.com

Page 226
Top left/Bottom left/right: Design created by Dal-Tile; 214-398-1411; www.daltile.com Top right: Design created by Florida Tile; 800-789-TILE; www.floridatile.com

Page 227
Top left: Design created by Florida Tile; 800-789-TILE; www.floridatile.com Top right/Bottom: Design created by Dal-Tile; 214-398-1411; www.daltile.com

Pages 228-229
All: Design created by Lori Carroll & Associates; 520-886-3443; www.loricarroll.com

Page 230
All: Design created by Imperial Home Décor Group; 888-608-5943; www.ihdg.com

Page 231
Top left/right/Bottom left: Design created by Imperial Home Décor Group; 888-608-5943; www.ihdg.com Bottom right: Design created by Seabrook Wallcoverings; 800-238-9152; www.seabrookwallcoverings.com

Page 232
Top left: Design created by Imperial Home Décor Group;

888-608-5943; www.ihdg.com Top right: Design created by New England Classic; 888-880-6324; www.newenglandclassic.com Bottom: Design created by German Sonntag; 310-452-2757

Page 233
Top: Design created by Lafia/Arvin, A Design Corporation; 310-587-1141; www.lafiaarvin.com Bottom left: Design created by New England Classic; 888-880-6324; www.newenglandclassic.com Bottom right: Design created by Dal-Tile; 214-398-1411; www.daltile.com

Page 234
Top left: Design created by Seabrook Wallcoverings; 800-238-9152; www.seabrookwallcoverings.com Top right/Bottom left/right: Design created by Imperial Home Décor Group; 888-608-5943; www.ihdg.com

Page 235
Top left/Bottom left: Design created by Imperial Home Décor Group; 888-608-5943; www.ihdg.com Top right/Bottom right: Design created by Seabrook Wallcoverings; 800-238-9152; www.seabrookwallcoverings.com

Page 236
Top: Design created by Leslie Harris Interior Design; 323-651-1422; www.leslieharrisinteriors.com Bottom left: Design created by Lori Carroll & Associates; 520-886-3443; www.loricarroll.com Bottom right: Design created by Rink Reynolds Diamond Fisher Wilson PA; 904-396-6353; www.rrdfw.com

Page 237
Top left (both): Design created by Lori Carroll & Associates; 520-886-3443; www.loricarroll.com Top right (both): Designs created by Interior Spaces, Inc; 310-399-4033; www.interiorspacesinc.com Bottom: Design created by

Leslie Harris Interior Design; 323-651-1422; www.leslieharrisinteriors.com

Page 238

Top left/Bottom left: Design created by Lori Carroll & Associates; 520-886-3443; www.loricarroll.com
Top right: Design created by Cheryl Gardner Interior Design; 323-856-0812; www.cherylgardner.com
Bottom right: Design created by Bonnie Sachs; 310-306-4595; www.bonniesachs.com

Page 239

Top left/right: Design created by Kari Whitman Interiors; 310-652-8684; www.kariwhitmaninteriors.com
Bottom: Design created by Sharon Sanchez; 727-692-7126; www.absolutedesign.org

Page 240

Top left: Design created by Seabrook Wallcoverings; 800-238-9152; www.seabrookwallcoverings.com
Top right/Bottom: Design created by Imperial Home Décor Group; 888-608-5943; www.ihdg.com

Page 241

All: Design created by Imperial Home Décor Group; 888-608-5943; www.ihdg.com

Page 242

Design created by Valspar; 800-845-9061; www.valspar.com

Page 243

All: Design created by Glidden, an ICI Paints brand; 800-GLIDDEN; www.glidden.com

Page 244

Top left/right: Design created by Glidden, an ICI Paints brand; 800-GLIDDEN; www.glidden.com
Bottom: Design created by Valspar; 800-845-9061; www.valspar.com

Page 245

Top: Design created by Valspar; 800-845-9061; www.valspar.com
Bottom left/right: Design created by Glidden, an ICI Paints brand; 800-GLIDDEN; www.glidden.com

Page 246

Top left/right: Design created by Seabrook Wallcoverings; 800-238-9152; www.seabrookwallcoverings.com
Bottom left/right: Design created by Imperial Home Décor Group; 888-608-5943; www.ihdg.com

Page 247

All: Design created by Imperial Home Décor Group; 888-608-5943; www.ihdg.com

Page 248

Top: Design created by Cheryl Gardner Interior Design; 323-856-0812; www.cherylgardner.com
Bottom left/center: Design created by Cultured Stone Corp.; 800-255-1727; www.culturedstone.com
Bottom right: Design created by El Dorado Stone; 800-925-1491; www.eldoradostone.com

Page 249

Top left/Bottom right: Design created by El Dorado Stone; 800-925-1491; www.eldoradostone.com
Top right/Center right: Design created by Cultured Stone Corp.; 800-255-1727; www.culturedstone.com

Pages 250-251

All: Design created by Imperial Home Décor Group; 888-608-5943; www.ihdg.com

Page 252

Top/Bottom center: Design created by Florida Tile; 800-789-TILE; www.floridatile.com
Bottom left/right: Design created by Dal-Tile; 214-398-1411; www.daltile.com

Page 253

Design created by Dal-Tile; 214-398-1411; www.daltile.com

Page 254

Top left/right/Bottom left: Design created by Imperial Home Décor Group; 888-608-5943; www.ihdg.com
Bottom right: Design created by Seabrook Wallcoverings; 800-238-9152; www.seabrook-wallcoverings.com

Page 255

Top left/Bottom left: Design created by Seabrook Wallcoverings; 800-238-9152; www.seabrookwallcoverings.com
Top right/Bottom right: Design created by Imperial Home Décor Group; 888-608-5943; www.ihdg.com

Page 256

Left: Design created by Rink Reynolds Diamond Fisher Wilson PA; 904-396-6353; www.rrdfw.com
Top right/Bottom right: Design created by New England Classic; 888-880-6324; www.newenglandclassic.com
Center right: Design created by Interior Spaces, Inc; 310-399-4033; www.interiorspacesinc.com

Page 257

Top left/Bottom right: Design created by New England Classic; 888-880-6324; www.newenglandclassic.com
Top right/Bottom left: Design created by The Wood Gallery, Inc; 812-923-8585; www.woodgallery.com

Page 258

Top left/right: Design created by Imperial Home Décor Group; 888-608-5943; www.ihdg.com
Top center/Bottom: Design created by Seabrook Wallcoverings; 800-238-9152; www.seabrookwallcoverings.com

Page 259

Top/Bottom right: Design created by Seabrook Wallcoverings; 800-238-9152; www.seabrookwallcoverings.com
Bottom left: Design created by Imperial Home Décor Group; 888-608-5943; www.ihdg.com

Pages 260-261

All: Design created by The Cheesecake Factory; www.cheesecakefactory.com

Page 262

Top left: BNK Design Consultants; 610-941-2943; www.BNKdesign.com
Bottom left: Design courtesy of Janna Colaco
Top right: Design created by Leslie Harris Interior Design; 323-651-1422; www.leslieharrisinteriors.com
Center right: Design created by Lori Carroll & Associates; 520-886-3443; www.loricarroll.com

Bottom right: Design created by New England Classic; 888-880-6324; www.newenglandclassic.com

Page 263

Top left: Design created by Lori Carroll & Associates; 520-886-3443; www.loricarroll.com
Top right: Design created by Lafia/Arvin, A Design Corporation; 310-587-1141; www.lafiaarvin.com
Center right: Design created by Bonnie Sachs; 310-306-4595; www.bonniesachs.com
Bottom right: Design created by Karen Brown Interiors, Inc; 813-340-2085

Contributing Photographers

Pages 111 (top), 114, 150, 168, 178, 196 (bottom/both), 262 (bottom left): Adam Crocker; 818-645-9600; adamcrocker@adelphia.net

Page 177 (top left): Van Fleet Photography; 562-225-5289; www.vanfleetphotography.com

Pages 148-149 (all), 238 (top right), 248 (top): Jeff Johnson; 612-339-7929; www.jeffjohnsonphoto.com

Page 179 (bottom): Michael Kalla; 323-962-1920; www.michaelkalla.com

Pages 233 (top), 263 (top right): Charles White; 323-937-3117; www.cswphoto.com

---

Contributing Artists

Page 239 (bottom): Daniel Acosta

Pages 1, 2-3, 191, 239 (top left/right): Artworks

Image Credit

Page 14 (top): The J. Paul Getty Museum, Los Angeles; Jules Degoullons; Paneling; about 1720; oak, carved, painted and gilded; 10ft.
Page 15 (bottom): The J. Paul Getty Museum, Los Angeles; Jacques Gaultier; Paneling; 1725-1726; painted and gilded wood, brèche d'Alep mantelpiece, modern mirrored glass; 13x26.9x22ft.

Glossary Of Terms

A

Abstract - A pattern or design not based on normal design ideas.

Acanthus - A motif based on the acanthus leaf. The design originated in Greece, where it was used on the capitals of the Corinthian columns.

Accent Wall – One wall of a room specifically designed to be the focus, often calling attention away from the other walls through the use of a fireplace or other imposing element (See Illustration).

Aerosol – The use of compressed gas to spray paint onto a wall.

All-Over Pattern – An effect produced by the repetition of a smaller pattern over an entire wall.

American Single Roll - A quantity of wallpaper between 34 and 36 square feet. The width of the roll is usually 20.5 inches, however, it can be up to 36 inches wide. The length ranges from 4 to 7 yards. (Compare to metric single roll).

Applique - A design technique where a cutout of one material is applied to the surface of another.

Arabesque - A pattern or style that uses flowers, foliage, fruit or sometimes animal and human figures to produce an intricate pattern of interlaced lines.

Art Deco – A design style from the 1920s and 1930s that emphasizes rounded, stylized motifs.

Art Nouveau – This "new art" style focuses on swirling lines, such as plant stems and tendrils.

B

Bandbox Designs – This design is based on motifs taken from early 18th century hatboxes and bandboxes, which were often covered with topical wallpaper.

Basket-weave Designs – Loosely woven fabric that is made to imitate the weave of a basket or wallpaper that gives a basket-weave effect.

Batik – A geometric type design from East India, often with a tie-dyed background.

Beidermeier - A neoclassic style which embodies simplicity and comfort.

Body – The consistency of a paint.

Bolt - A continuous roll of wallpaper, packaged as one unit. It contains a quantity of paper equivalent to two single rolls.

Booking – The process of folding wallcoverings to make for easier handling when applying paste.

Borders – A decorative strip of wallpaper that can be used at the chair rail, baseboard, around doors and windows, or at the ceiling line. Borders often correspond with the main wallpaper of a wall.

Butted Seam – A point at which two pieces of wallpaper touch, but do not overlap.

C

Caen-stone – A wallcovering designed to resemble cream colored stone that can be found in Caen, France.

Cartouche - A motif shaped as an unrolled scroll, often with an inscription or other emblematic decoration.

Cellulose - A type of wallpaper paste generally used for non-vinyl wallcovering.

Chalk line – A chalk line is used to establish a vertical plumb line on a wall, so as to properly align paper on the wall.

Chinoiserie – A design label that is loosely applied to almost any oriental form of decoration.

Chintz - Papers resembling printed cotton material, from India, with the same name, featuring brightly colored flowers.

Collage – A technique combining pictures with patterns and other, often textured, materials.

Companion Wallcoverings – A set of wall coverings specifically designed to be integrated together to create an overall design.

Corduroy – Wall coverings that imitate corduroy fabric.

Country – A resurging style that became popular in the 1970s, country employs calico, quilted and gingham patterns to create a nostalgic tone.

Crewel Work – Full color hand embroidered wall coverings, originating in India, that use native designs such as the tree of life.

Crown Molding - Molding or trim that lines the top of a room, usually right up to the ceiling.

D

Dado – The amount of usable wall space between a chair rail and the baseboard.

Damask - Patterns that imitate stylized textiles usually containing floral, foliage or swag themes, among others.

Deglosser – A liquid which, when applied to a high gloss paint, causes the paint to look flatter.

Directional Print - A pattern or wallpaper designed with the specific intention of being installed in a certain direction to achieve the desired effect.

Double Cutting – This is a technique that is often used to make a perfect seam when using non matching wallcoverings. The two wallcoverings are overlapped by two inches and then cut down the middle with a razor. The overlapping flaps are then removed and the seam then fits perfectly.

Drier – An agent that aids in the drying of a coat of paint.

Drop Cloth – Any kind of cloth put down to keep paint or glue from getting onto the existing floor.

E

Eclectic – An inclusion of many different styles from different places and periods.

Embossing – Gives a wall covering a raised effect by impressing a design into the material with either heat or pressure.

Enamel – Paint that forms a hard, smooth film and is usually oil-based.

F

Fabric Wall - A wall entirely covered in fabric. A fabric wall can contain one type of fabric or many types incorporated into a pattern or design (See Illustration).

Flame Stitch – This style, adapted from Hungarian needlework stitch, features multicolored patterns.

Fleur-de-lis – The fleur-de-lis was a stylized iris flower adopted by French kings as a royal symbol.

Flocked – Flocked walls have small flecks of very fine cotton, silk, rayon or nylon stuck in the paint to create a three dimensional effect.

Floral Print – Any pattern or style that includes recognizable flowers and foliage.

Fluting – Parallel, carved depressions in wood or stone, or wall coverings that imitate a long, groove.

Focal Point – The major point of interest in a room, such as the fire place.

Fret – A border motif that is made up of geometrically interlocking lines.

G

Gloss - The ability of painted surface to reflect light. The higher the gloss, the more scrubbable and durable the finish. Degrees of gloss include flat, velvet, eggshell, low lustre, semi-gloss and high gloss.

Granite – A very hard, igneous rock consisting of feldspar, quartz, and other minerals. Granite is very resistant to damage, but requires some periodic care.

Grasscloth – Originating in Japan, grasscloth was often actual grasses or vines glued to a backing, but now refers also to wallpapers imitating this style.

Grotesque – This motif stretches the imagination with various distortions of the forms of human beings, animals, or plants.

H

Harlequin – Diamond shapes arranged into different patterns.

Header Strip – A particular type of border wall covering that is designed to be placed above a door or window.

Hemp – This wallpaper is designed in the same fashion as grasscloth but employs fibers from the hemp plant for a much finer weave.

Heraldic – Designs that focus upon some form of family or heraldry, such as a coat of arms.

J

Jacobean – Jacobean is a combination of crewel work

originating in Indian, and Elizabethean and Tudor styles.

Jaspe – This type of wall covering is named for its reproduction of jasper stone cut across the grain.

Jute - Wallpaper designed like grasscloth, but with the much coarser weave acquired through the use of jute fibers.

L

Leather Paper – Wallpaper that, through heavy embossing and varnishing, takes upon the appearance of leather.

Limestone – A very porous, sedimentary rock consisting mainly of calcite.

Linen – Wallcoverings made of linen are noted for their fine weave and textile resemblance.

M

Marble – Marble is a metamorphic rock formed from limestone that is very common in architecture and sculpture.

Marble Patterns – Patterns made to look like marble.

Masking Tape – Easily removable tape that is used to cover areas that should not be painted.

Matching – Properly laying two sheets of wallpaper so that the pattern lines up correctly.

Matte Finish - A dull finish.

Metallics – Paints that contain metal flakes.

Metric Single Roll - A metric roll contains 28 to 30 square feet per single roll. It is usually 21 inches wide and 16 feet long, or can be 27 inches wide and 13 feet long. Also known as a euro roll. (Compare to American single roll).

Mission – This style is based upon the Southern California Spanish missions, and the southwestern flair they contain.

Monk's Cloth – A rough weave of coarse cotton yarns.

Monochromatic – One color, or possibly different tones of one color.

Mosaic – A type of wall covering that uses small pieces of glass, stone and tile set in cement to form a pattern.

Motif – A recurring design in a piece or set of wallpaper.

Mural – A mural is a large pictorial design created often from paint or wallpaper that covers an entire wall or room.

Mylar – Mylar is a material that looks like foil and is added to a wall covering to create that shiny feel as well as add durability.

O

Oil Paints – Paints with an oil base. This means that they must be thinned with a paint thinner. Also called alkyd paints.

Ombre - Striped wall coverings or fabrics of one color in several tones.

Outside Corner - A corner formed when two walls, not facing each other, are joined.

P

Paisley – Paisley is a comma-shaped motif named after the town of its origin, Paisley, Scotland.

Pearl Finish – A finishing coat that gives a pearly shine to wallpaper or paint.

Pilaster - A flat column superimposed on any plain surface as a support of cornice or pediment.

Pillement Design - Named for Jean Pillement, this style incorporates floral designs with Oriental styles.

Plaid - Designs consisting of crossed stripes, many of them originating in Scottish tartans.

Prepasted – Prepasted wallpaper is paper that comes with paste already on the backing. The paste is usually activated by soaking in water for instructed lengths of time.

Primer – Paint or acrylic applied to a wall before a final coat of paint or a wallcovering. This gives the wall a uniform base that makes for better adhesion of both paint and other wallcoverings.

Provincial – Refers to designs inspired by European and colonial American arts and crafts.

R

Railroading – When wallpaper is applied in horizontal stripes as opposed to vertical stripes.

Random Match – Wallpaper that does not depend on matching different panels of paper to achieve an aesthetic effect.

Recoat Time – The amount of time that is required for a coat of paint to dry before another can be applied.

Relief – A design that is more prominent due to being raised above the normal plane of the paper, often through embossing. Another example of relief is designs incorporating wood carving (See Illustration).

Repeat - The distance from the center of one motif of a

pattern to the center of the next.

Roller – A tool that is used to apply paint by soaking and then rolling onto a wall. Rollers can be made of different types of fabric or foam.

Rosette – A motif containing leaves and petals arranged around a central point.

S

Sandstone – A sedimentary rock composed of sand and quartz.

Seam Roller – A small tool that is used once the wallpaper is applied to the wall to remove any air bubbles and flatten any seams. It should not be used with grasscloth, embossed papers, flocked papers and other wallpapers with similar substances.

Selvage – The edges of a roll of wallpaper that are left blank and are used to protect the wallpaper.

Shade - A color produced by adding black to a pigment.

Shading – Shading occurs when wallpaper printing causes tonal differences from one side of a sheet of paper to another. Reversing every other strip of wallpaper can remedy this problem.

Shiki - Hand-made Oriental silk glued to a backing.

Sizing – A powder that is mixed with water and then applied to the wall surface to increase the adhesion of a wallpaper.

Slate – A compact, metamorphic rock that can be split into slabs or plates.

Slip – The amount of sliding that can be done to a piece of wallpaper during installation, once it has been applied to a wall.

Small Scale Pattern – Patterns with small designs and smaller distances between repeats of that design.

Smoothing Brush – This brush is used to smooth out wrinkles and air bubbles during installation of wallpaper.

Soffit – The area of the wall that extends from the top of a cabinet or shelf to the ceiling.

Soirette – A wall covering that is an accurate reproduction of silk fabric.

Sponge – A sponge is used to clean off wet paste that may have smeared during wallpaper installation.

Straight Edge – A ruler or other straight edge that is used to make sure any trimming has a perfectly straight line.

Straight Match – A pattern match where the pattern is the same all the way across the wall.

Strie - A thread-like, striped effect.

Substrate – Substrate is the backing that is glued to a wall. Substrates can be made out of almost any type of material.

Swatch - A sample.

T

Tea Chest Paper – A style that used small, geometrical patterns and is based on designs from paper that was used to package tea in the Orient.

Tint - A color produced when a pigment is mixed with white.

Trellis Design - Lattice-work, sometimes supporting climbing flowers.

Tromp L'oeil – Meaning, literally, to fool the eye, tromp l'oeil designs use shadow to create a three-dimensional illusion.

Tudor Rose – An English motif combining the white rose of York and the red rose of Lancaster.

U

Unpasted Wallpaper – Wallpaper that has not been prepasted by the manufacturer.

V

Varnish – A compound that gives a clear or translucent finish.

W

Wainscoting – Paneling or woodwork that covers the dado of a wall, or the bottom third of the wall.

Wall Liner – Also known as liner paper, wall liner is stock wallpaper used for the purpose of covering cracks and imperfections before applying wallpaper or water-based paint. Wall liner also reduces the risk of mildew as it absorbs moisture. It is also good preparation for murals and the installation of metallic wallpapers.

Waterbox – A tray containing water into which prepasted wallpaper is dipped to activate the paste for installation.

Wet Hanging – A method of wallpaper hanging where paste is applied to the back of unpasted wallpaper and then the paper is applied to the wall.

Wood Paneling– The raised, recessed or framed part of a wooden wall (See Illustration).

Index

Arches 178, 200-201

Art 194-195, 213, 263

Backyards 119, 139, 253

Baroque 12-15

Bathrooms 1, 6-7, 32, 37, 41, 44, 49, 55, 58, 63, 79, 95, 102-103, 116-117, 124-125, 132-133, 140-141, 143, 154, 175, 179, 193, 198-199, 207, 225-228, 231, 238, 247, 251

Bedrooms 32-34, 36-37, 40, 44, 47-48, 50, 52, 54-58, 60-64, 69, 76, 78-83, 85-87, 96-98, 104, 108, 138, 142, 146, 180-181, 185, 189, 194-195, 210-211, 215-217, 220-221, 224, 234-235, 237-238, 240, 244-246, 254-255, 258, 263-264, 270

Brick 190

Broken Marble 262

Built-In Aquarium 177

Children's Rooms 42-43, 78, 82-83, 189, 216, 238, 244-245, 254-255

Chippendale, Thomas 16

Creative Architecture 178-179, 200-201, 236-237

Creative Furnishings 186-187

Creative Room Division 212-213

Dining Rooms 47, 49-50, 77, 88-89, 96, 106-107, 149, 151-3, 155, 162, 164, 167, 172-173, 175-176, 178, 186-187, 189, 212-213, 215, 219, 224, 225, 230, 233, 237, 239-242, 256, 258, 263

Eastlake, Charles 31

Eclectic Fusion 204-205, 260-261

Elevators 237

Empire 24-27

English Renaissance 10-11

Fabric 184-185

Faux Finish 2-3, 177, 191, 198-199, 238-239

Federal 24-27

Fireplaces 36, 49-50, 84, 115, 119-121, 127, 130-131, 134-135, 138-139, 143, 145, 159, 168-172, 177, 182, 196, 206, 208, 217, 222-223, 226, 230, 232-234, 241, 243, 248-249, 258, 262-263

Foyers 81, 108, 110, 148, 152, 160, 163, 191, 201, 203, 229, 249, 252

French Renaissance 10

Frescoes 13

Fresquera 10

Frieze 31

Georgian 16-23

Hallways 118, 134, 148, 175, 204

Historical Illustrations 8-31, 280-283

Japanese Screens 193

Kitchens 60, 68, 90, 111-113, 115, 120, 122-123, 128-129, 135-7, 221-222, 226-227, 230, 235-236, 245-248, 250

Living Rooms 2-3, 35-36, 38-39, 45, 46, 48-53, 59, 64-68, 70-75, 84, 90-96, 98-101, 104-105, 109, 111, 114-115, 119-122, 127, 130-131, 134, 138-9, 143-5, 150, 153, 159, 161, 163, 164, 168, 170, 172, 177, 179, 182-186, 190, 195-197, 200-202, 209, 213, 219, 222-223, 230, 232-237, 239-241, 243, 245, 248-249, 259, 262-263

Log Walls 182-183

Media Room 196

Murals 188-189, 202-203, 237

Neoclassic 20-23

Paint 1, 2-3, 76-109, 164-165, 174, 190, 216-219, 238-239, 242-245, 270-275

Palladio, Andrea 16

Plasma Televisions 196-197, 262

Quadrilateral Design 208-209

Regency 24-27

Renaissance 8-11

Rococo 16-19

Sculpture 177

Spanish Renaissance 10

Shelving 176, 202

Stairways 126, 153, 166, 170, 193, 217, 219, 256-257, 259, 262

Stone 110-111, 114-115, 118-119, 122-123, 126-127, 130-131, 134-135, 138-139, 222-223, 248-249

Study 144, 156-157, 160, 225

Tapestries 263

Tile 110-113, 116-117, 120-121, 124-125, 128-129, 132-133, 136-137, 140-141, 226-229, 252-253

Victorian 28-31

Wall Flowering 180-181, 206-207

Wallpaper 6-7, 10-11, 14, 17, 19, 22-23, 27-29, 31, 32-75, 175, 188-189, 202-203, 214-215, 220-221, 224-225, 230-231, 234-235, 240-241, 246-247, 250-251, 254-255, 258-259, 264-269

Wine Cellar 248

Wood Carving 209

Wood Paneling 8-31, 142-175, 232-233, 256-257

Bibliography

Authentic Decor:
The Domestic Interior
Peter Thornton
Seven Dials, Cassell & Co., 2000

Paint Your Home
Francis Donegan
The Reader's Digest Association, Inc., 1997

Wallpaper in America: From the Seventeenth Century to World War I
Catherine Lynn
W.W. Norton & Company, 1980

Complete Paint & Wall Coverings Sunset, 1999

Nineteenth Century Interiors:
An Album of Watercolours
Charlotte Gere
Thames and Hudson, 1992

The Complete Guide to Wallpapering
David M. Groff
Creative Homeowner, 1999

The Elements of Style:
Revised Edition
Stephen Calloway and Elizabeth Cromley
Simon & Schuster, 1991

Curtains & Drapes
Jenny Gibbs
Cassell, 1994